Skills for Scholars

MW01232547

GRADE 3

Spanish

Frank Schaffer Publications®

Printed in the United States of America. All rights reserved. Limited Reproduction Permission: Permission to duplicate these materials is limited to the person for whom they are purchased. Reproduction for an entire school or school district is unlawful and strictly prohibited. Frank Schaffer Publications is an imprint of School Specialty Publishing. Copyright © 2006 School Specialty Publishing.

Send all inquiries to:
Frank Schaffer Publications
3195 Wilson Drive NW
Grand Rapids, Michigan 49534

Spanish—Grade 3

ISBN 0-7696-8243-X

1 2 3 4 5 6 7 8 9 10 WAL 10 09 08 07 06

Table of Contents

Numbers Crossword

Use the words at the bottom to help you with this crossword puzzle. Write the Spanish number words in the puzzle spaces. Follow the English clues.

ACROSS

1. three
2. ten
3. fifteen
6. twenty
7. six
9. eight
12. four
13. nine
15. twelve

DOWN

1. thirteen
4. fourteen
5. five
7. seven
8. one
10. eleven
11. zero
14. two

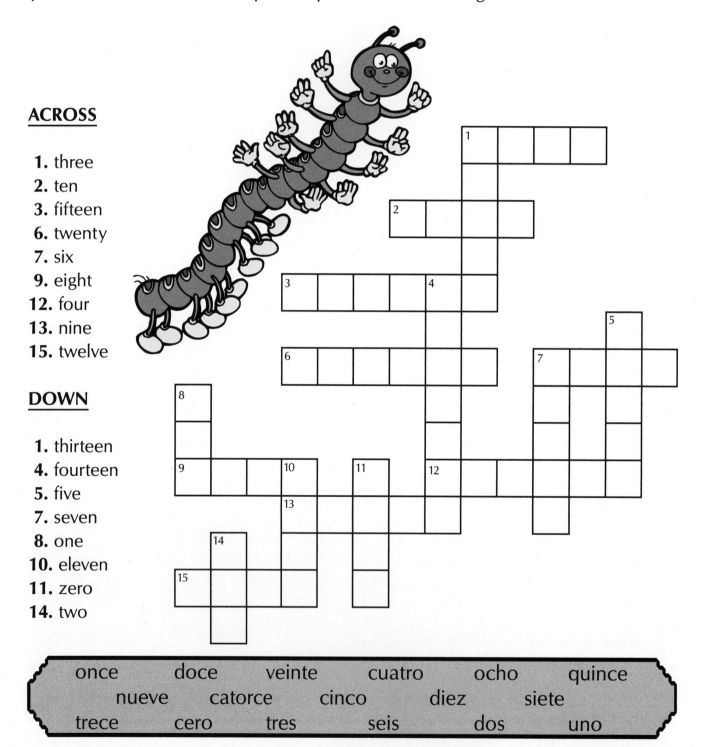

once	doce	veinte	cuatro	ocho	quince
nueve	catorce	cinco	diez	siete	
trece	cero	tres	seis	dos	uno

Numbers

After each numeral, write the number word in Spanish. Refer to the words below to help you.

Word Bank

veinte	cuatro	nueve	diez	diecisiete	quince
doce	once	trece	siete	uno	tres
catorce	dos	cero	ocho	cinco	dieciséis
diecinueve		dieciocho		seis	

0 _____

1 _____

2 _____

3 _____

4 _____

5 _____

6 _____

7 _____

8 _____

9 _____

10 _____

11 _____

12 _____

13 _____

14 _____

15 _____

16 _____

17 _____

18 _____

19 _____

20 _____

Numbers Illustration

Write the number. Draw that many things in the box. The first one is done for you.

★ ★ ★ ★ ★ ★ ★ ★ **ocho** means __8__	**cinco** means _____	**diecisiete** means _____
doce means _____	**uno** means _____	**dos** means _____
catorce means _____	**nueve** means _____	**veinte** means _____
siete means _____	**cuatro** means _____	**quince** means _____

Who Is It?

Write the names of people you may know that fit each description below.

tú–informal or familiar form of you	
someone you refer to by first name	
your sister or brother (or cousin)	
a classmate	
a close friend	
a child younger than yourself	

usted–formal or polite form of you	
someone with a title	
an older person	
a stranger	
a person of authority	

How would you speak to each person below? Write *tú* or *usted* after each person named.

1. Dr. Hackett _____

2. Susana _____

3. a four-year-old _____

4. your grandfather _____

5. the governor _____

6. your best friend _____

7. your sister _____

8. the principal _____

9. a classmate _____

10. a stranger _____

Masculine and Feminine

All Spanish nouns and adjectives have gender. This means they are either masculine or feminine. Here are two basic rules to help determine the gender of words. There are other rules for gender which you will learn as you study more Spanish.

1. Spanish words ending in -o are usually masculine.

2. Spanish words ending in -a are usually feminine.

Write the following words in the charts to determine their gender. Write the English meanings to the right. Use a Spanish-English dictionary if you need help.

maestra	libro	escritorio	negro	abrigo	sopa	tienda
amigo	ventana	pluma	maestro	vestido	fruta	museo
silla	puerta	anaranjado	amiga	camisa	queso	casa
rojo	cuaderno	blanco	falda	chaqueta		

Masculine		Feminine	
words ending in -o	meaning of the word	words ending in -a	meaning of the word

It's a Small World

In Spanish, there are four ways to say "the"—*el, la, los,* and *las.* The definite article (the) agrees with its noun in gender (masculine or feminine) and number (singular or plural).

Masculine singular nouns go with *el.* Feminine singular nouns go with *la.*

Examples: *el libro* (the book)   *el papel* (the paper)
la silla (the chair)   *la regla* (the ruler)

Masculine plural nouns go with *los.* Feminine plural nouns go with *las.*

Examples: *los libros* (the books)   *los papeles* (the papers)
las sillas (the chairs)   *las reglas* (the rulers)

Refer to the Word Bank to complete the chart. Write the singular and plural forms and the correct definite articles. The first ones have been done for you.

Word Bank				
cuaderno	mesa	pluma	oso	falda
papel	gato	bota	silla	libro

English	Masculine Singular	Masculine Plural
the book	*el libro*	*los libros*
the paper		
the notebook		
the cat		
the bear		

English	Feminine Singular	Feminine Plural
the chair	*la silla*	*las sillas*
the table		
the boot		
the skirt		
the pen		

Pretty Colors

Adjectives are words that tell about or describe nouns. Color each box as indicated in Spanish. Use a Spanish-English dictionary if you need help.

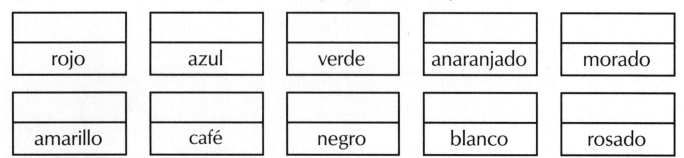

rojo	azul	verde	anaranjado	morado

amarillo	café	negro	blanco	rosado

Here are some new adjectives. Copy the Spanish adjectives in the boxes. Write the Spanish words next to the English at the bottom of the page.

bonita	pretty	feo	ugly
grande	big	pequeño	small
limpio	clean	sucio	dirty
viejo	old	nuevo	new
alegre	happy	triste	sad

old _____   pretty _____   sad _____

big _____   small _____   happy _____

new _____   dirty _____   ugly _____

clean _____

10   *Spanish: Grade 3*

Words to Describe

Descriptive adjectives are words that describe nouns. Refer to the Word Bank to write the Spanish adjective that describes each picture.

Word Bank					
alegre	grande	nuevo	pequeño	feo	rico
limpio	sucio	bonita	triste	viejo	pobre
alto	bajo	abierto	cerrado		

large	new	ugly	happy
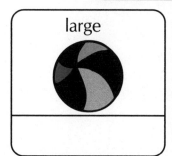			

old	sad	small	clean
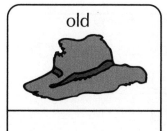		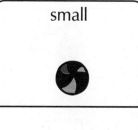	

pretty	dirty	tall	open

rich	short	closed	poor
	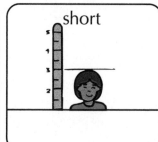		

Words to Describe

Write the Spanish words for the clue words in the crossword puzzle.

Across

3. poor
7. open
9. tall
11. clean
12. dirty
13. new

Down

1. ugly
2. closed
4. happy
5. pretty
6. large
8. old
10. sad

Word Bank

viejo	grande
limpio	nuevo
bonita	triste
abierto	cerrado
alto	sucio
pobre	alegre
feo	

Action Words

In each box, copy the Spanish action verbs. Then, write the English word below it.

comer		hablar	
_____		_____	
_____		_____	
beber		limpiar	
_____		_____	
_____		_____	
dormir		mirar	
_____		_____	
_____		_____	
tocar		dar	
_____		_____	
_____		_____	

Word Bank

to touch	to look at	to eat	to give
to drink	to speak	to clean	to sleep

Name _____

Action Figures

Write the Spanish words from the Word Bank that fit in these word blocks. Write the English below the blocks.

Word Bank

mirar	limpiar	tocar	beber
hablar	comer	dar	dormir

1.

_____

2.

_____

3.

_____

4.

_____

5.

_____

6.

_____

7.

_____

8.

_____

English

to eat	to look at	to speak	to touch
to clean	to sleep	to drink	to give

Greetings Paste Up

Cut out a picture from a magazine that shows the meaning of each greeting and glue it next to the correct word or words.

¡Hola!

¿Cómo te llamas?

Me llamo...

¿Cómo estás?

bien

mal

así, así

¡Adiós!

Name _____

What's Your Name?

Refer to the Word Bank to translate the Spanish questions and answers into English.

1. ¿Cómo te llamas? _____

   Me llamo _____. _____

2. ¿Cómo estás? _____

   Estoy bien/mal/así así. _____

3. ¿Cuántos años tienes? _____

   Tengo ___ años. _____

Write the English meaning after the Spanish word.

4. hola _____   8. por favor _____

5. amigo, amiga _____   9. gracias _____

6. sí _____   10. ¡Hasta luego! _____

7. no _____   11. adiós _____

Word Blocks

Write the Spanish words from the Word Bank that fit in these word blocks. Don't forget the punctuation. Write the English meanings below the blocks.

1. 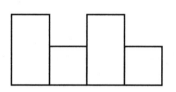   2.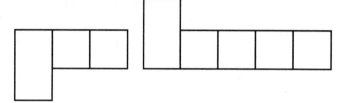

_____   _____

3. 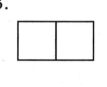   4.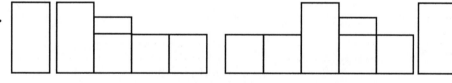

_____   _____

5.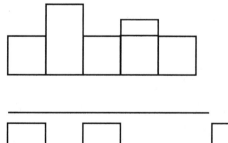

_____

6.

_____

7.

_____

Spanish Word Bank

por favor   adiós   Estoy bien.
hola   ¡Hasta luego!   ¿Cómo te llamas?
no   ¿Cómo estás?

8.

_____

Name _____ Spanish: _____

Greetings

Write the English meaning of the Spanish words and phrases.

1. señor _____

2. señora _____

3. señorita _____

4. maestro _____

5. maestra _____

6. ¡Buenos días! _____

7. ¡Buenas tardes! _____

8. ¡Buenas noches! _____

9. Vamos a contar. _____

Word Bank

Mr.	Good night!	Good morning!
Good afternoon!	teacher (female)	teacher (male)
Miss	Let's count.	Mrs.

Draw a picture to show the time of day that you use each expression.

¡Buenos días!	¡Buenas tardes!	¡Buenas noches!

Name _____

Spanish Greetings

Write the Spanish word for each clue in the crossword puzzle.

Across

1. bad
4. good
7. teacher (male)
9. friend (female)
10. Mr.
11. Miss

Down

2. friend (male)
3. hello
5. thank you
6. goodbye
7. teacher (female)
8. Mrs.

Word Bank

amiga	mal
señora	señor
maestra	bien
adiós	hola
señorita	gracias
amigo	maestro

Yesterday and Today

Write the Spanish words for the days of the week. Remember, in Spanish-speaking countries, Monday is the first day of the week.

Word Bank

miércoles	jueves	sábado
viernes	lunes	martes
	domingo	

Monday _____

Tuesday _____

Wednesday _____

Thursday _____

Friday _____

Saturday _____

Sunday _____

If today is Monday, yesterday was Sunday. Complete the following chart by identifying the missing days in Spanish. The first one is done for you.

ayer (yesterday)	hoy (today)	mañana (tomorrow)
martes	miércoles	jueves
lunes		
		sábado
	domingo	
	jueves	
		martes
viernes		

Rain in April

Refer to the Word Bank to write the Spanish word for the given month. Then, in the box, draw a picture of something that happens in that month of the year. Remember that Spanish months do not begin with capital letters.

Word Bank

agosto	septiembre	noviembre	mayo
junio	enero	octubre	febrero
marzo	julio	diciembre	abril

January _____		July _____	
February _____		August _____	
March _____		September _____	
April _____		October _____	
May _____		November _____	
June _____		December _____	

21 *Spanish: Grade 3*

Writing Practice

Copy the following paragraph in your best handwriting. Practice reading it out loud.

Hay doce meses en un año. Diciembre, enero y febrero son en el invierno. Marzo, abril y mayo son en la primavera. Junio, julio y agosto son en el verano. Septiembre, octubre y noviembre son en el otoño. ¿Cuál es tú favorito mes del año?

_____

_____

_____

_____

_____

_____

_____

_____

_____

_____

Name _____

Birds of Color

Color the birds according to the words listed.

azul
café
morado
rosado
rojo
verde
negro
amarillo
anaranjado

House of Colors

Color each crayon with the correct color for the Spanish word. Add something with your favorite color.

☐ rojo ☐ negro ☐ café ☐ rosado
☐ azul ☐ amarillo ☐ blanco ☐ verde

Name _____

Color the Flowers

Color each flower with the correct color for the Spanish word.

☐ azul ☐ café ☐ amarillo ☐ rosado
☐ verde ☐ rojo ☐ morado ☐ anaranjado

Moving Colors

Color the pictures according to the words listed.

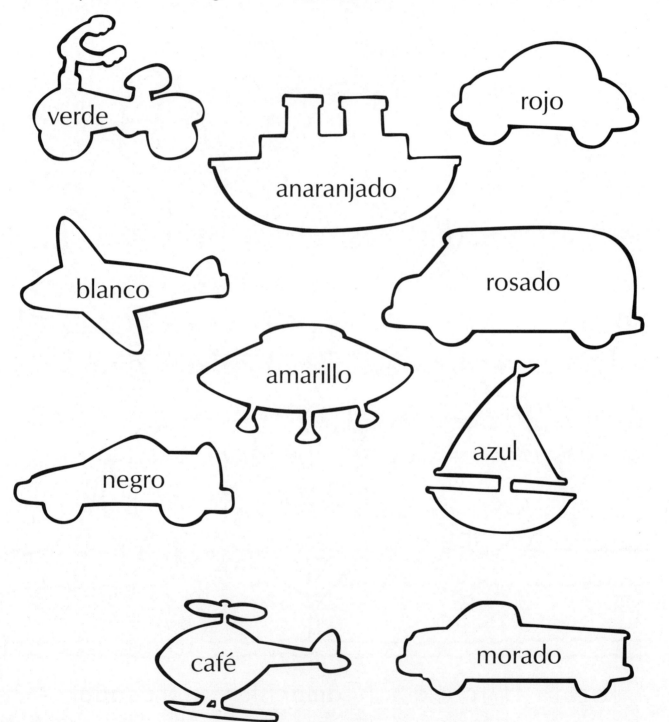

verde

anaranjado

rojo

blanco

rosado

amarillo

negro

azul

café

morado

What is your favorite color? (Answer in Spanish.) _____

Color Crossword

Write the correct Spanish color words in the spaces.
Follow the English color clues.

ACROSS

3. yellow

5. purple

6. black

8. white

10. pink

DOWN

1. blue

2. red

4. orange

7. green

9. brown

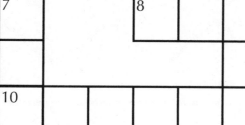

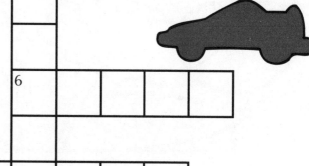

blanco	rojo	anaranjado	verde	rosado
azul	morado	amarillo	café	negro

Colorful Flowers

Color the flowers according to the Spanish color words shown.

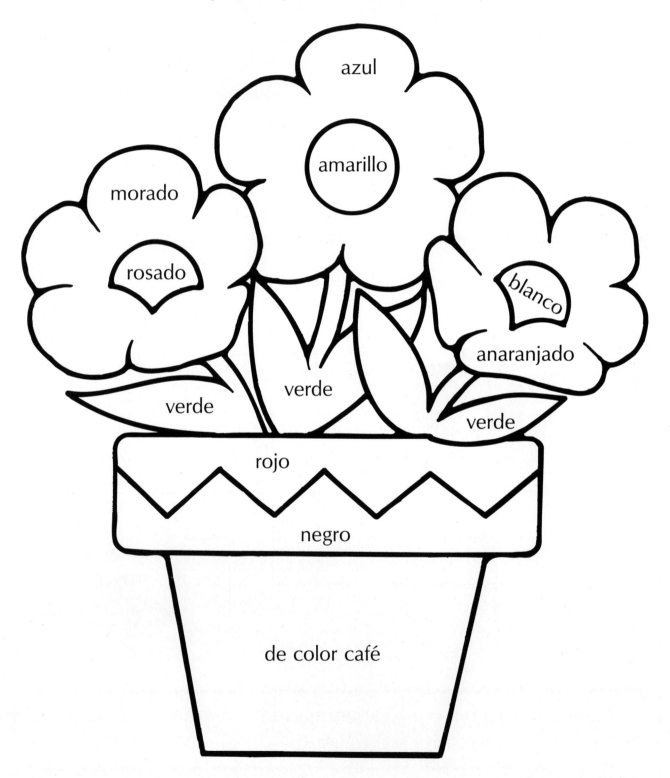

azul

amarillo

morado

rosado

blanco

anaranjado

verde

verde

verde

rojo

negro

de color café

Draw and Color

In each box, write the Spanish color word. Use the Word Bank below to help you. Then, draw and color a picture of something that is usually that color.

red is _____	orange is _____	brown is _____
blue is _____	purple is _____	black is _____
green is _____	yellow is _____	pink is _____

Which Spanish color from the Word Bank is not used above? _____

Word Bank

blanco	rojo	amarillo	rosado
azul	morado	verde	negro
	anaranjado	café	

Butterfly Garden

Color the butterfly garden as indicated in Spanish.

Name _____

Across the Spectrum

Write the Spanish for each clue word in the crossword puzzle.

Across

2. blue
4. brown
6. red
7. purple
8. white
9. black

Down

1. green
2. yellow
3. pink
5. orange

Food Words

Say each word out loud. Write the English word next to it.

queso _____

leche _____

papa _____

jugo

pan _____

pollo _____

ensalada _____

Color the blocks with letters.
Do not color the blocks with numbers. What word did you find? _____

7	x	7	7	7	7	7	7	7	7	7	x	7	7	7	7	7	7	7
7	x	7	7	7	7	7	7	7	7	7	x	7	7	7	7	7	7	7
7	x	7	7	7	7	7	7	7	7	7	x	7	7	7	7	7	7	7
7	x	7	x	x	x	7	x	x	x	7	x	7	7	7	x	x	x	7
7	x	7	x	7	x	7	x	7	7	7	x	x	x	7	x	7	x	7
7	x	7	x	x	x	7	x	7	7	7	x	7	x	7	x	x	x	7
7	x	7	x	7	7	7	x	7	7	7	x	7	x	7	x	7	7	7
7	x	7	x	x	x	7	x	x	x	7	x	7	x	7	x	x	x	7

Spanish: Grade 3

Food Riddles

Answer the riddles. Use the size and shape of the word blocks along with the answers at the bottom to help you.

I come from an animal. Kids like to eat my drumstick. What am I?

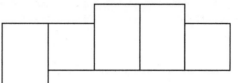

I can be full of holes. Mice like me. What am I?

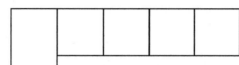

I am squeezed from fruit. Apple is a popular flavor. What am I?

I come from a cow. I can be regular or chocolate. What am I?

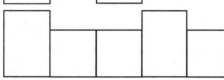

You can eat me baked, fried, or mashed. What am I?

You can eat me plain or with dressing. What am I?

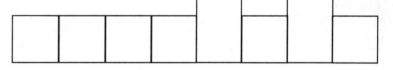

I rise while baking in an oven. What am I?

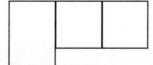

queso   leche

papa   ensalada   pan

pollo   jugo

Use the Clues

Use the clues and the Word Bank at the bottom of the page to find the answers.
Do not use any answer more than once.

1. You would not eat either of these fruits until you peel them.

_____   _____

2. Both of these drinks have a flavor.

_____   _____

3. You could put either of these on a sandwich.

_____   _____

4. These can be baked before eating. They all begin with the letter "p."

_____   _____   _____

5. These two go together on a cold winter day.

_____   _____

6. You use this liquid to wash this fruit.

_____   _____

7. Which word didn't you use?

_____

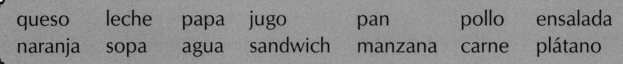

| queso | leche | papa | jugo | pan | pollo | ensalada |
| naranja | sopa | agua | sandwich | manzana | carne | plátano |

Check off each word as you use it.

34   *Spanish: Grade 3*

A Square Meal

Refer to the Word Bank to write the name of each food in Spanish.

Word Bank

queso	vegetales
leche	naranja
papa	sopa
pan	agua
jugo	sandwich
pollo	manzana
ensalada	carne
fruta	plátano

Eat It Up

Write the Spanish for the clue words in the crossword puzzle.

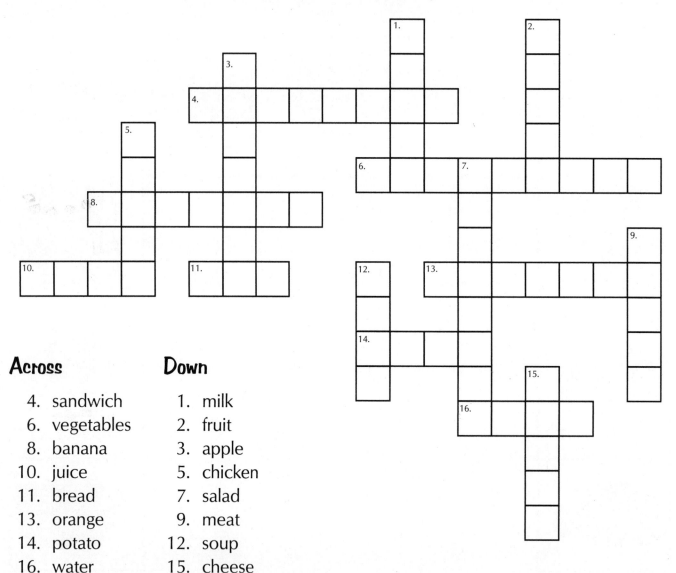

Across

4. sandwich
6. vegetables
8. banana
10. juice
11. bread
13. orange
14. potato
16. water

Down

1. milk
2. fruit
3. apple
5. chicken
7. salad
9. meat
12. soup
15. cheese

Word Bank

ensalada	plátano	manzana	papa
pan	naranja	fruta	queso
carne	sopa	jugo	vegetales
sandwich	leche	agua	pollo

Use the Clues

Answer the questions. Use the clues and the Spanish words at the bottom of the page. You may use answers more than once.

1. Both words begin with the same letter, and both animals have feathers.

_____ _____

2. These two animals walk and are house pets.

_____ _____

3. Both animals begin with the same letter. One quacks and the other barks.

_____ _____

4. Both of these animals like to live in the water.

_____ _____

5. These animals do not have fur or feathers.

_____ _____

6. The first animal likes to chase and catch the second animal. They both end with the letter o.

_____ _____

gato	perro	pájaro
pez	pato	culebra

Name _____

Three Little Kittens

Draw a picture to match the Spanish phrase in each box.

seis pájaros	cuatro perros
nueve abejas	siete osos
tres gatos	dos vacas
cinco patos	ocho caballos
diez ranas	un pez

Name _____

Animal Match

Copy the Spanish word under each picture.

oso	rana	caballo	vaca

_____	_____	_____	_____

elefante	oveja	puerco	gallina

_____	_____	_____	_____

gato	tortuga	mariposa	dinosaurio

_____	_____	_____	_____

Write the Spanish for each animal name.

1. butterfly _____

2. sheep _____

3. cat _____

4. dinosaur _____

5. chicken _____

6. pig _____

7. cow _____

8. bear _____

9. elephant _____

10. horse _____

11. turtle _____

12. frog _____

Clothes to Color

Cut out pictures and glue them next to the correct words.

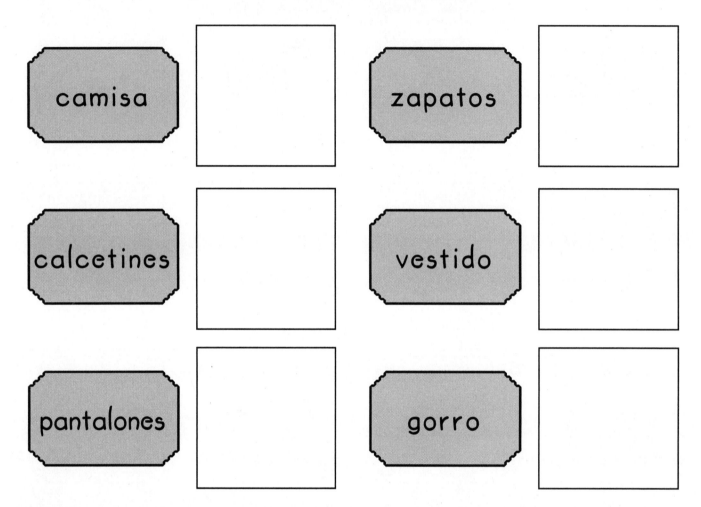

camisa

zapatos

calcetines

vestido

pantalones

gorro

Try this: Color each block with a letter X inside. Do not color the blocks with numbers. What hidden word did you find? _____

8	8	8	8	8	8	8	8	8	8	8	8	8	8	8	8	8	8	8	8	8	8	8
8	8	x	x	x	8	x	x	x	8	x	x	x	8	x	x	x	8	x	x	x	8
8	8	x	8	x	8	x	8	x	8	x	8	x	8	x	8	x	8	x	8	x	8
8	8	x	x	x	8	x	8	x	8	x	8	8	8	x	8	8	8	x	8	x	8
8	8	8	8	x	8	x	x	x	8	x	8	8	8	x	8	8	8	x	x	x	8
8	8	x	8	x	8	8	8	8	8	8	8	8	8	8	8	8	8	8	8	8	8
8	8	x	x	x	8	8	8	8	8	8	8	8	8	8	8	8	8	8	8	8	8

Clothes Closet

Refer to the Word Bank and write the Spanish word for each item of clothing pictured.

Word Bank			
vestido	calcetines	botas	zapatos
sombrero	cinturón	falda	chaqueta
guantes	pantalones cortos	pantalones	camisa

shirt	
shorts	
socks	
shoes	
boots	
gloves	

pants	
hat	
skirt	
belt	
dress	
jacket	

41   *Spanish: Grade 3*

Dressing Up

Write the Spanish word for each clue in the crossword puzzle.

Word Bank

cinturón	botas	camisa
guantes	calcetines	sombrero
chaqueta	falda	zapatos
pantalones	vestido	

Across

1. shoes
4. socks
7. dress
8. gloves
9. hat
10. shirt

Down

2. pants
3. skirt
4. jacket
5. belt
6. boots

Matching Clothes

At the bottom of each picture, write the English word that matches the Spanish and the pictures. Write the Spanish words next to the English at the bottom of the page.

falda	zapatos	pantalones cortos	cinturón
abrigo	calcetines	vestido	botas
guantes	pantalones	chaqueta	blusa
gorro	sandalias	camisa	

1. skirt _____

2. belt _____

3. jacket _____

4. socks _____

5. coat _____

6. shirt _____

7. sandals _____

8. dress _____

9. cap _____

10. pants _____

11. gloves _____

12. boots _____

13. shoes _____

14. blouse _____

15. shorts _____

Face Riddles

Can you guess the answers to the following riddles? Use the size and shape of the letter blocks to write the Spanish word. The answers at the bottom will help you.

There are two of me. Sometimes I need glasses. What am I?

I like to be washed and combed. What am I?

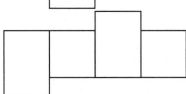

I help hold up glasses. When I feel an itch, I sneeze. What am I?

Everyone's looks a little different, in spite of the shape. What am I?

We grow, get loose, fall out, and grow again. What are we?

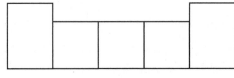

"Open wide" is often said when I am too small. What am I?

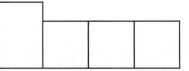

Does your mom always tell you to wash behind us? What are we?

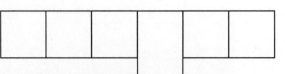

nariz   pelo   dientes
ojos   orejas   cara   boca

Name _____

A Blank Face

Fill in the blanks with the missing letters. Use the Spanish words below to help you.

| nariz | pelo | dientes | ojos | orejas | cara | boca |

Which word didn't you use? _____

Color each block that has a letter k inside. Do not color the blocks with numbers.
What hidden word did you find? _____

k	5	5	5	5	5	5	5	5	5	5	5	5	5	5	5
k	5	5	5	5	5	5	5	5	5	5	5	5	5	5	5
k	5	5	5	5	5	5	5	5	5	5	5	5	5	5	5
k	k	k	5	k	k	k	5	k	k	k	5	k	k	k	5
k	5	k	5	k	5	k	5	k	5	5	5	k	5	k	5
k	5	k	5	k	5	k	5	k	5	5	5	k	5	k	5
k	k	k	5	k	5	k	5	k	k	k	5	k	k	k	k

Name _____

How Are You?

Label each facial feature with a Spanish word from the Word Bank.

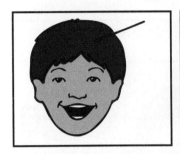  

_____ _____ _____

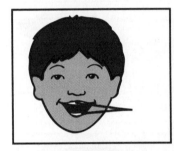  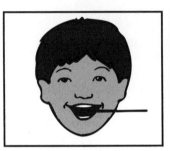 

_____ _____ _____ _____

Copy the Spanish word that matches each face pictured.

happy	sad	crying
	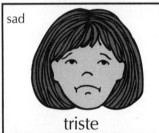	
alegre	triste	llorando

_____ _____ _____

smiling	angry	thinking
	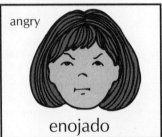	
sonriendo	enojado	pensando

_____ _____ _____

Happy Faces

Write the Spanish for the clue words in the crossword puzzle.

Across

1. sad
3. nose
5. eyes
6. thinking
8. face
11. smiling
13. crying

Down

2. angry
4. happy
7. teeth
9. ears
10. mouth
12. hair

Word Bank

llorando	orejas	sonriendo	ojos
pelo	nariz	triste	cara
dientes	alegre	enojado	boca
pensando			

Matching Family

Cut out a picture of a family out of a magazine. Glue each picture next to the correct word.

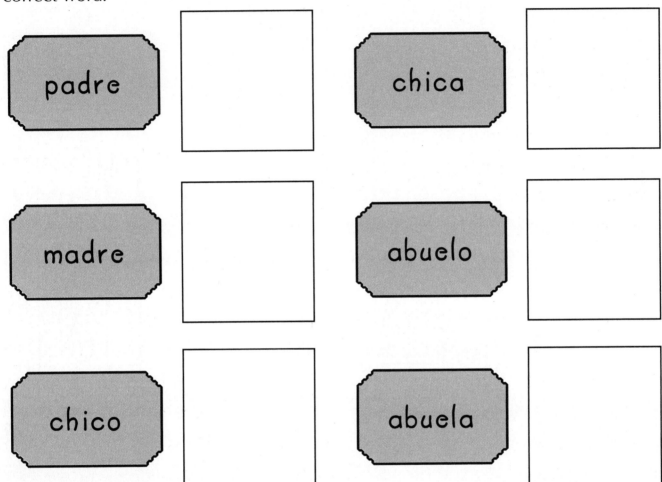

padre		chica	
madre		abuelo	
chico		abuela	

Try this: Color each block with a letter inside. Do not color the blocks with numbers.

What hidden word did you find? _____

2	2	2	2	2	2	2	2	2	2	2	2	2	m	2	2	2	2	2	2	2
2	2	2	2	2	2	2	2	2	2	2	2	2	m	2	2	2	2	2	2	2
m	m	m	m	m	2	m	m	m	2	2	m	m	m	2	m	m	m	2	m	m	m
m	2	m	2	m	2	m	2	m	2	2	m	2	m	2	m	2	m	2	m	2	m
m	2	m	2	m	2	m	2	m	2	2	m	2	m	2	m	2	2	2	m	m	m
m	2	m	2	m	2	m	2	m	2	2	m	2	m	2	m	2	2	2	m	2	2
m	2	m	2	m	2	m	m	m	m	2	m	m	m	2	m	2	2	2	m	m	m

48 *Spanish: Grade 3*

Family Ties

In each box, copy the Spanish word for family members.

la familia	family	el hermano	brother
el padre	father	la hermana	sister
la madre	mother	el tío	uncle
el hijo	son	la tía	aunt
la hija	daughter	el abuelo	grandfather
los primos	cousins	la abuela	grandmother

Write the Spanish words from above next to the English words.

sister _____   family _____   father _____

grandfather _____   cousins _____   mother _____

grandmother _____   brother _____   daughter _____

uncle _____   aunt _____   son _____

My Family

Write the Spanish word for each clue in the crossword puzzle.

Across

2. son
3. aunt
5. sister
7. grandmother
8. brother
10. cousins

Down

1. mother
2. daughter
4. family
6. grandfather
9. uncle
10. father

Word Bank

familia	hermano	hijo	tía
primos	madre	tío	abuelo
padre	hermana	hija	abuela

Family Tree

Refer to the Word Bank to write the Spanish word that matches each picture.

family

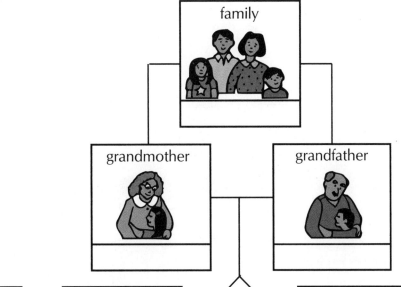

grandmother

grandfather

mother

father

aunt

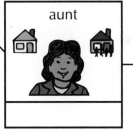

uncle

son

daughter

cousins

brother

sister

Name _____

Places, Please

Cut out pictures that match the words below. Glue each picture next to the correct word.

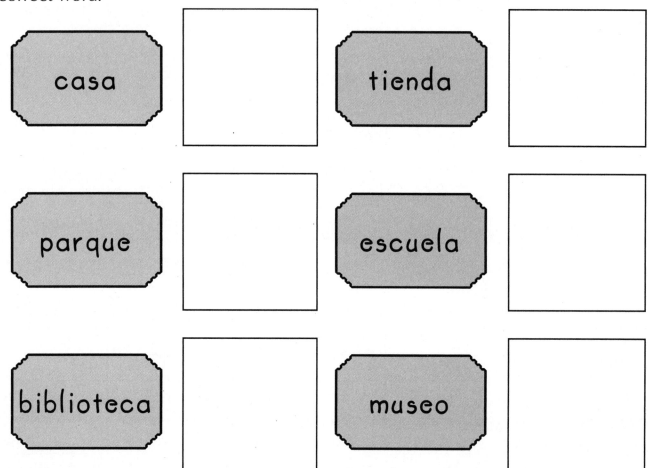

casa

tienda

parque

escuela

biblioteca

museo

Try this: Color each block with a letter Y inside. Do not color the blocks with numbers. What hidden word did you find? _____

9	9	9	9	9	9	9	9	9	9	9	9	9	9	9	9	9
y	y	y	9	y	y	y	9	9	y	y	y	9	y	y	y	9
y	9	y	9	y	9	y	9	9	y	9	9	9	y	9	y	9
y	9	9	9	y	9	y	9	9	y	y	y	9	y	9	y	9
y	9	y	9	y	9	y	9	9	9	9	y	9	y	9	y	9
y	y	y	9	y	y	y	y	9	y	y	y	9	y	y	y	y
9	9	9	9	9	9	9	9	9	9	9	9	9	9	9	9	9

A Place for Riddles

Answer the riddles. Use the size and shape of the letter blocks to write the Spanish words. The answers at the bottom of the page will help you.

People live in me.
What am I?

If you want to buy something, you come to me. What am I?

People like to come to me for playing and relaxing. What am I?

I am filled with books that you can borrow. What am I?

I am filled with children, desks, and books. What am I?

I often have dinosaur bones. What am I?

Dinosaurios

| escuela | museo | casa |
| biblioteca | tienda | parque |

Name _____

Where Am I?

Refer to the Word Bank and write the Spanish for each place in the community pictured.

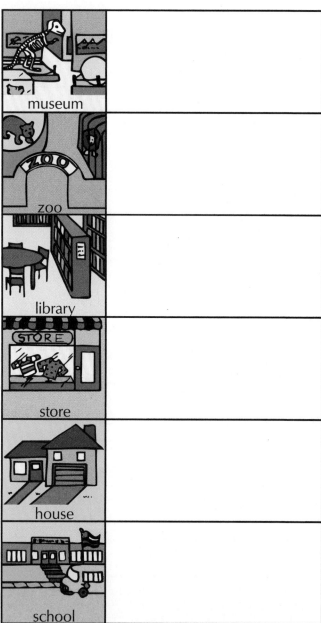

Word Bank	

escuela	granja	biblioteca	tienda
museo	casa	apartamento	zoológico
iglesia	restaurante	cine	parque

Fitting In

Write the Spanish words from the Word Bank in these word blocks. Write the English meanings below the blocks.

1.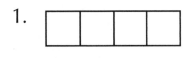

_____

2.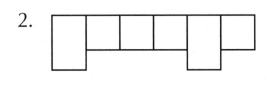

_____

3.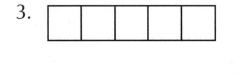

_____

4.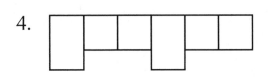

_____

5.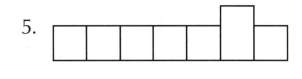

_____

6.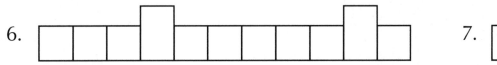

_____

7.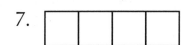

_____

8.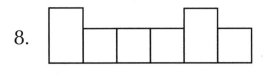

_____

9.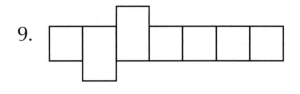

_____

10.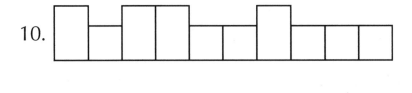

_____

Around the House

Copy the Spanish words. Then, write the English words below them.

casa

_____

_____

cocina

_____

_____

sala

_____

_____

dormitorio

_____

_____

sofá

_____

_____

cama

_____

_____

lámpara

_____

_____

cuchara

_____

_____

Word Bank

couch	kitchen	lamp	spoon
bedroom	bed	house	living room

Around the Block

Write the Spanish words from the Word Bank that fit in these word blocks. Write the English below the blocks.

Word Bank

casa	dormitorio	lámpara
cocina	sofá	cuchara
sala	cama	

1.

_____

2.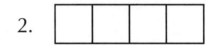

_____

3.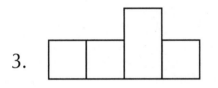

_____

4.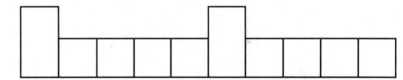

_____

5.

_____

6.

_____

7.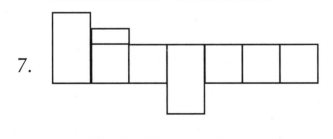

_____

8.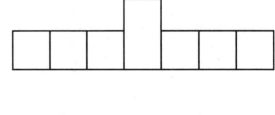

_____

Around the House

Write the Spanish words for the clue words in the crossword puzzle.

Across

2. kitchen
3. lamp
5. towel
8. living room
9. telephone
11. stove

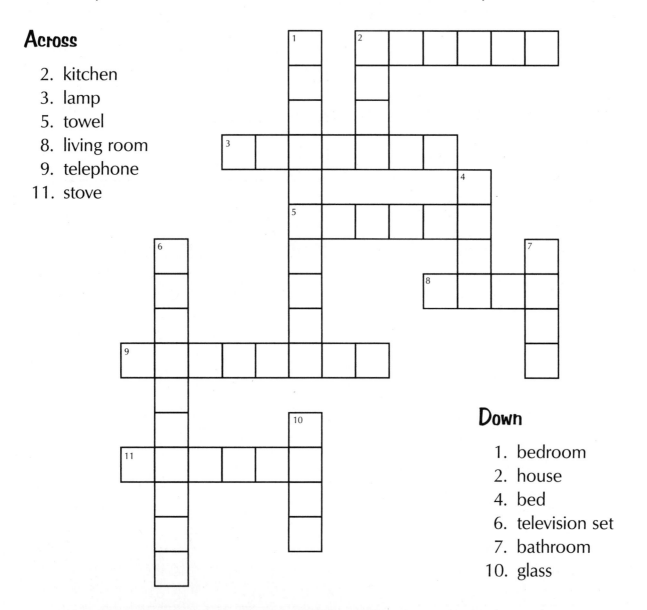

Down

1. bedroom
2. house
4. bed
6. television set
7. bathroom
10. glass

Word Bank

baño	cocina	lámpara	televisión
dormitorio	teléfono	toalla	cama
vaso	casa	estufa	sala

Match Words and Pictures

Cut out pictures from a magazine and glue each picture next to the correct word.

silla

borrador

mesa

lápiz

tijeras

libro

Use the Clues

Use the clues and the words at the bottom of the page. Do not use any answer more than once.

1. Both words begin with the letter *p*. You write <u>with</u> one and write <u>on</u> one. What are they?

_____   _____

2. You can sit at either one of these when you need to write.

_____   _____

3. You could exit through either one of these in case of fire.

_____   _____

4. Both words end with the letter *o*. They both have pages.

_____   _____

5. These two words go together because one is on the end of the other.

_____   _____

6. Both words have an *i* as their second letter. One is used for cutting and the other is used for sitting.

_____   _____

silla	mesa	tijeras	libro	borrador	ventana
puerta	lápiz	cuaderno	papel	escritorio	pluma

Around the Room

In each box, copy the Spanish word for the classroom object pictured.

silla		mesa	
puerta		pluma	
ventana		borrador	
lápiz		cuaderno	
papel		libro	
escritorio		tijeras	

Write the Spanish words from above next to the English words.

window _____   chair _____   table _____

eraser _____   scissors _____   door _____

desk _____   pen _____   notebook _____

paper _____   book _____   pencil _____

A Fitting Design

Write the Spanish words from the Word Bank that fit in these word blocks. Write the English meanings below the blocks.

Word Bank			
ventana	papel	pluma	puerta
borrador	silla	libro	cuaderno
escritorio	tijeras	mesa	lápiz

1.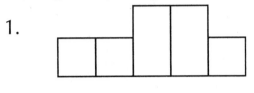

2.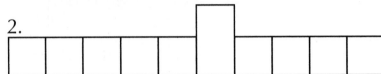

3.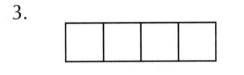

4.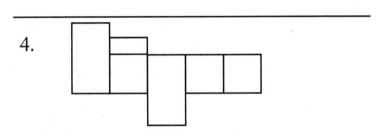

5.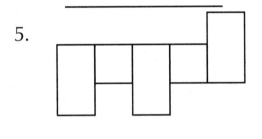

6.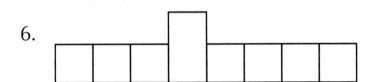

7.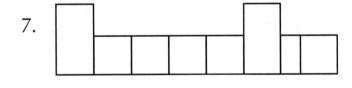

8.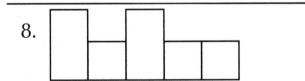

9.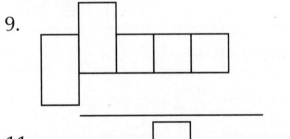

10.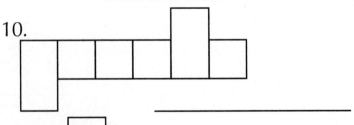

11.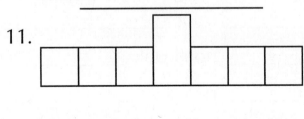

12.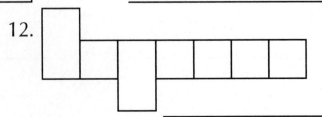

Classroom Clutter

Draw a picture to illustrate each of the Spanish words. Refer to the Word Bank at the bottom of the page to help you.

silla	*ventana*
mesa	*puerta*
tijeras	*papel*
libro	*cuaderno*
lápiz	*escritorio*
borrador	*pluma*

Word Bank

eraser	door	scissors	pen	window	paper
chair	notebook	pencil	desk	book	table

Show and Tell

Write the Spanish for each clue in the crossword puzzle.

Across

1. notebook
5. scissors
7. pen
8. eraser
10. pencil
11. table
12. chair

Down

2. desk
3. window
4. book
6. door
9. paper

Word Bank

escritorio   mesa   libro   silla   tijeras   puerta
lápiz   ventana   borrador   cuaderno   papel   pluma

Songs and Chants

Food Song

(to the tune of "She'll Be Coming 'Round the Mountain")

Queso is cheese, yum, yum, yum. (clap, clap)
Leche is milk, yum, yum, yum. (clap, clap)
Papa is potato.
Jugo is juice.
Pan is bread, yum, yum, yum! (clap, clap)

Pollo is chicken, yum, yum, yum. (clap, clap)
Ensalada is salad, yum, yum, yum. (clap, clap)
Queso, leche, papa,
jugo, pan, pollo, ensalada,
yum, yum, yum, yum, yum! (clap, clap)

Community Song

(to the tune of "Here We Go 'Round the Mulberry Bush")

Escuela is school,   museo museum;
casa is house,   tienda is store;
biblioteca is library;   parque is the park for me!

Songs

¡Hola, chicos!

(to the tune of "Goodnight Ladies")

¡Hola, chico! ¡Hola, chica!
¡Hola, chicos! ¿Cómo están hoy?
¡Hola, chico! ¡Hola, chica!
¡Hola, chicos! ¿Cómo están hoy?

Los días de la semana

(to the tune of "Clementine")

Domingo, lunes,
martes, miércoles,
jueves, viernes, sábado,
domingo, lunes,
martes, miércoles,
jueves, viernes, sábado. (Repitan)

66

Name_____

Learning Cards

levántense	**cierren**
siéntense	**cállensen**
abran	**póngansen**

Published by Frank Schaffer Publications. Copyright protected. **67** *Spanish: Grade 3*

Learning Cards

close	**stand up**
be quiet	**sit down**
line up	**open**

Learning Cards

párense	**pinten**
corten	**dibujen**
peguen	**canten**

Learning Cards

paint	**stop**
draw	**cut**
sing	**paste**

Numbers Crossword

Use the words at the bottom to help you with this crossword puzzle. Write the Spanish number words in the puzzle spaces. Follow the English clues.

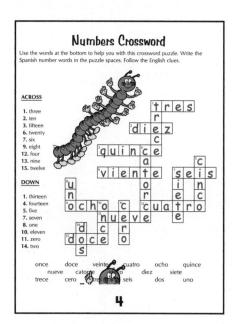

ACROSS
1. three
2. ten
3. fifteen
6. twenty
7. six
9. eight
12. four
13. nine
15. twelve

DOWN
1. thirteen
4. fourteen
5. five
7. seven
8. one
10. eleven
11. zero
14. two

Crossword answers: tres, diez, quince, viente, seis, uno, ocho, cuatro, nueve, doce (plus down letters: trece, catorce, cinco, siete, once, cero, dos)

once   doce   veinte   cuatro   ocho   quince
nueve   catorce   diez   siete
trece   cero   tres   seis   dos   uno

4

Numbers

After each numeral, write the number word in Spanish. Refer to the words below to help you.

Word Bank

veinte	cuatro	nueve	diez	diecisiete	quince
doce	once	trece	siete	uno	tres
catorce	dos	cero	ocho	cinco	dieciséis
diecinueve		dieciocho		seis	

0 cero
1 uno
2 dos
3 tres
4 cuatro
5 cinco
6 seis
7 siete
8 ocho
9 nueve
10 diez

11 once
12 dos
13 trece
14 catorce
15 quince
16 dieciséis
17 diecisiete
18 dieciocho
19 diecinueve
20 veinte

5

Numbers Illustration

Write the number. Draw that many things in the box. The first one is done for you.

Pictures Will Vary.

★★★★ ★★★★ ocho means _8_	cinco means _5_	diecisiete means _17_
doce means _12_	uno means _1_	dos means _2_
catorce means _14_	nueve means _9_	veinte means _20_
siete means _7_	cuatro means _4_	quince means _15_

6

Who Is It?

Write the names of people you may know that fit each description below.

tú–informal or familiar form of you	
someone you refer to by first name	
your sister or brother (or cousin)	
a classmate	*Answers Will Vary.*
a close friend	
a child younger than yourself	

usted–formal or polite form of you	
someone with a title	
an older person	
a stranger	*Answers Will Vary.*
a person of authority	

How would you speak to each person below? Write *tú* or *usted* after each person named.

1. Dr. Hackett usted
2. Susana tú
3. a four-year-old tú
4. your grandfather usted
5. the governor usted
6. your best friend tú
7. your sister tú
8. the principal usted
9. a classmate tú
10. a stranger usted

7

Masculine and Feminine

All Spanish nouns and adjectives have gender. This means they are either masculine or feminine. Here are two basic rules to help determine the gender of words. There are other rules for gender which you will learn as you study more Spanish.

1. Spanish words ending in -o are usually masculine.
2. Spanish words ending in -a are usually feminine.

Write the following words in the charts to determine their gender. Write the English meanings to the right. Use a Spanish-English dictionary if you need help.

maestra	libro	escriturio	negro	abrigo	sopa	tienda
amigo	ventana	pluma	maestro	vestido	fruta	museo
silla	puerta	anaranjado	amiga	camisa	queso	casa
rojo	cuaderno	blanco	falda	chaqueta		

Masculine		**Feminine**	
words ending in -o	meaning of the word	words ending in -a	meaning of the word
amigo	friend (male)	maestra	teacher (female)
rojo	red	silla	chair
libro	book	ventana	window
cuaderno	notebook	puerta	door
escriturio	desk	pluma	pen
anaranjado	orange	amiga	friend (female)
museo	museum	falda	skirt
blanco	white	camisa	shirt
negro	black	chaqueta	jacket
maestro	teacher (male)	sopa	soup
abrigo	coat	fruta	fruit
vestido	dress	tienda	store
queso	cheese	casa	house

8

It's a Small World

In Spanish, there are four ways to say "the"–*el, la, los,* and *las.* The definite article (the) agrees with its noun in gender (masculine or feminine) and number (singular or plural).

Masculine singular nouns go with *el.* Feminine singular nouns go with *la.*

Examples: *el libro* (the book)   *el papel* (the paper)
la silla (the chair)   *la regla* (the ruler)

Masculine plural nouns go with *los.* Feminine plural nouns go with *las.*

Examples: *los libros* (the books)   *los papeles* (the papers)
las sillas (the chairs)   *las reglas* (the rulers)

Refer to the Word Bank to complete the chart. Write the singular and plural forms and the correct definite articles. The first ones have been done for you.

Word Bank	cuaderno	mesa	pluma	oso	falda
	papel	gato	bota	silla	libro

English	Masculine Singular	Masculine Plural
the book	el libro	los libros
the paper	el papel	los papeles
the notebook	el cuaderno	los cuadernos
the cat	el gato	los gatos
the bear	el oso	los osos

English	Feminine Singular	Feminine Plural
the chair	la silla	las sillas
the table	la mesa	las mesas
the boot	la bota	las botas
the skirt	la falda	las faldas
the pen	la pluma	las plumas

9

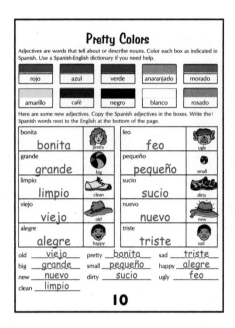

Pretty Colors

Adjectives are words that tell about or describe nouns. Color each box as indicated in Spanish. Use a Spanish-English dictionary if you need help.

rojo	azul	verde	anaranjado	morado
amarillo	café	negro	blanco	rosado

Here are some new adjectives. Copy the Spanish adjectives in the boxes. Write the Spanish words next to the English at the bottom of the page.

bonita	**bonita**	pretty	feo	**feo**	ugly
grande	**grande**	big	pequeño	**pequeño**	small
limpio	**limpio**	clean	sucio	**sucio**	dirty
viejo	**viejo**	old	nuevo	**nuevo**	new
alegre	**alegre**	happy	triste	**triste**	sad

old **viejo**   pretty **bonita**   sad **triste**
big **grande**   small **pequeño**   happy **alegre**
new **nuevo**   dirty **sucio**   ugly **feo**
clean **limpio**

10

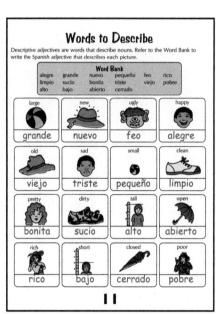

Words to Describe

Descriptive adjectives are words that describe nouns. Refer to the Word Bank to write the Spanish adjective that describes each picture.

Word Bank
alegre grande nuevo pequeño feo rico
limpio sucio bonita triste viejo pobre
alto bajo abierto cerrado

large **grande**	new **nuevo**	ugly **feo**	happy **alegre**
old **viejo**	sad **triste**	small **pequeño**	clean **limpio**
pretty **bonita**	dirty **sucio**	tall **alto**	open **abierto**
rich **rico**	short **bajo**	closed **cerrado**	poor **pobre**

11

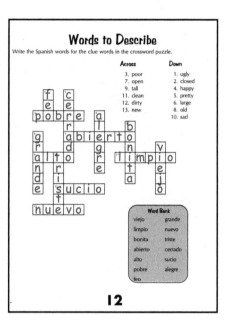

Words to Describe

Write the Spanish words for the clue words in the crossword puzzle.

Across
3. poor
7. open
9. tall
11. clean
12. dirty
13. new

Down
1. ugly
2. closed
4. happy
5. pretty
6. large
8. old
10. sad

(crossword grid with answers: feo, cerrado, pobre, alto, grande, triste, abierto, alegre, bonita, limpio, viejo, sucio, nuevo)

Word Bank
viejo grande
limpio nuevo
bonita triste
abierto cerrado
alto sucio
pobre alegre
feo

12

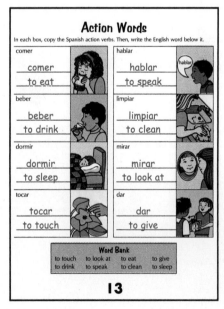

Action Words

In each box, copy the Spanish action verbs. Then, write the English word below it.

comer	hablar
comer / **to eat**	**hablar** / **to speak**
beber	limpiar
beber / **to drink**	**limpiar** / **to clean**
dormir	mirar
dormir / **to sleep**	**mirar** / **to look at**
tocar	dar
tocar / **to touch**	**dar** / **to give**

Word Bank
to touch to look at to eat to give
to drink to speak to clean to sleep

13

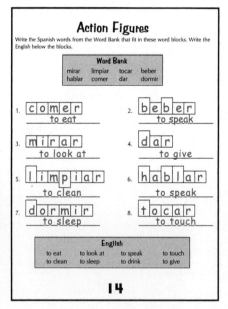

Action Figures

Write the Spanish words from the Word Bank that fit in these word blocks. Write the English below the blocks.

Word Bank
mirar limpiar tocar beber
hablar comer dar dormir

1. c o m e r — to eat
2. b e b e r — to speak
3. m i r a r — to look at
4. d a r — to give
5. l i m p i a r — to clean
6. h a b l a r — to speak
7. d o r m i r — to sleep
8. t o c a r — to touch

English
to eat to look at to speak to touch
to clean to sleep to drink to give

14

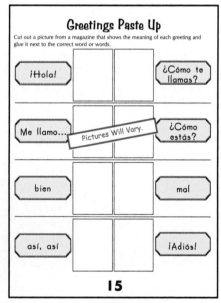

Greetings Paste Up

Cut out a picture from a magazine that shows the meaning of each greeting and glue it next to the correct word or words.

¡Hola!   ¿Cómo te llamas?

Me llamo...   *Pictures Will Vary.*   ¿Cómo estás?

bien   mal

así, así   ¡Adiós!

15

What's Your Name?

Word Bank

I'm so–so.	What's your name?	I'm well/fine.
I'm ___ years old.	I'm not doing well.	My name is ___
I'm so–so.	How are you?	How old are you?

Refer to the Word Bank to translate the Spanish questions and answers into English.

1. ¿Cómo te llamas? **What is your name?**

   Me llamo **My name is ___.**

2. ¿Cómo estás? **How are you?**

   Estoy bien/mal/así así. **I'm fine. I'm not well. I'm so-so.**

3. ¿Cuántos años tienes? **How old are you?**

   Tengo ___ años. **I am ___ years old.**

Word Bank

hello	please	friend	yes
no	thank you	goodbye	See you later!

Write the English meaning after the Spanish word.

4. hola **hello**
5. amigo, amiga **friend (m/f)**
6. sí **yes**
7. no **no**
8. por favor **please**
9. gracias **thank you**
10. ¡Hasta luego! **See you later!**
11. adiós **goodbye**

16

Word Blocks

Write the Spanish words from the Word Bank that fit in these word blocks. Don't forget the punctuation. Write the English meanings below the blocks.

1. h o l a — hello
   2. p o r   f a v o r — please
3. n o — no   4. ¡ H a s t a   l u e g o ! — See you later!
5. ¿ C ó m o   e s t á s ? — How are you?
6. ¿ C ó m o   t e   l l a m a s ? — What is your name?
7. a d i ó s — goodbye

Spanish Word Bank

por favor	adiós	Estoy bien.
hola	¡Hasta luego!	¿Cómo te llamas?
no		¿Cómo estás?

8. E s t o y   b i e n . — I am fine.

17

Greetings

Write the English meaning of the Spanish words and phrases.

1. señor **Mr.**
2. señora **Mrs.**
3. señorita **Miss**
4. maestro **teacher (male)**
5. maestra **teacher (female)**
6. ¡Buenos días! **Good morning!**
7. ¡Buenas tardes! **Good afternoon!**
8. ¡Buenas noches! **Good night!**
9. Vamos a contar. **Let's count**

Word Bank

Mr.	Good night!	Good morning!
Good afternoon!	teacher (female)	teacher (male)
Miss	Let's count.	Mrs.

Draw a picture to show the time of day that you use each expression.

¡Buenos días!	¡Buenas tardes!	¡Buenas noches!
Pictures Will Vary.		

18

Spanish Greetings

Write the Spanish word for each clue in the crossword puzzle.

Across
1. bad
4. good
7. teacher (male)
9. friend (female)
10. Mr.
11. Miss

Down
2. friend (male)
3. hello
5. thank you
6. goodbye
7. teacher (female)
8. Mrs.

Word Bank

amiga	mal
señora	señor
maestra	bien
adiós	hola
señorita	gracias
amigo	maestro

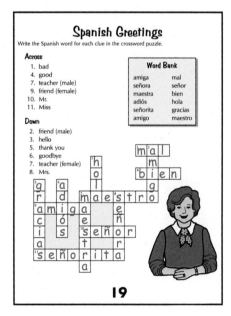

19

Yesterday and Today

Write the Spanish words for the days of the week. Remember, in Spanish-speaking countries, Monday is the first day of the week.

Word Bank

miércoles	jueves	sábado
viernes	lunes	martes
	domingo	

Monday	lunes
Tuesday	martes
Wednesday	miércoles
Thursday	jueves
Friday	viernes
Saturday	sábado
Sunday	domingo

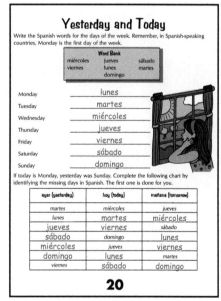

If today is Monday, yesterday was Sunday. Complete the following chart by identifying the missing days in Spanish. The first one is done for you.

ayer (yesterday)	hoy (today)	mañana (tomorrow)
martes	miércoles	jueves
lunes	martes	miércoles
jueves	viernes	sábado
sábado	domingo	lunes
miércoles	jueves	viernes
domingo	lunes	martes
viernes	sábado	domingo

20

Rain in April

Refer to the Word Bank to write the Spanish word for the given month. Then, in the box, draw a picture of something that happens in that month of the year. Remember that Spanish months do not begin with capital letters.

Word Bank

agosto	septiembre	noviembre	mayo
junio	enero	octubre	febrero
marzo	julio	diciembre	abril

January		July	
enero		julio	
February	Pictures Will Vary.	August	Pictures Will Vary.
febrero		agosto	
March		September	
marzo		septiembre	
April		October	
abril		octubre	
May		November	
mayo		noviembre	
June		December	
junio		diciembre	

21

Writing Practice

Copy the following paragraph in your best handwriting. Practice reading it out loud.

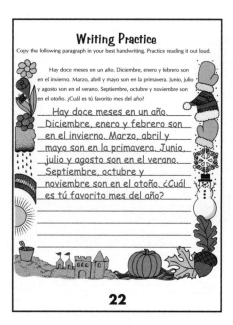

Hay doce meses en un año. Diciembre, enero y febrero son en el invierno. Marzo, abril y mayo son en la primavera. Junio, julio y agosto son en el verano. Septiembre, octubre y noviembre son en el otoño. ¿Cuál es tú favorito mes del año?

Hay doce meses en un año.
Diciembre, enero y febrero son
en el invierno. Marzo, abril y
mayo son en la primavera. Junio,
julio y agosto son en el verano.
Septiembre, octubre y
noviembre son en el otoño. ¿Cuál
es tú favorito mes del año?

22

Birds of Color

Color the birds according to the words listed.

azul
café
morado
rojo
rosado
verde
negro
amarillo
anaranjado

23

House of Colors

Color each crayon with the correct color for the Spanish word. Add something with your favorite color.

Pictures Will Vary.

■ rojo   ■ negro   ■ café   ■ rosado
■ azul   □ amarillo   □ blanco   ■ verde

24

Color the Flowers

Color each flower with the correct color for the Spanish word.

morado
amarillo
rojo
rosado
café
anaranjado
azul
verde

■ azul   ■ café   □ amarillo   ■ rosado
■ verde   ■ rojo   ■ morado   ■ anaranjado

25

Moving Colors

Color the pictures according to the words listed.

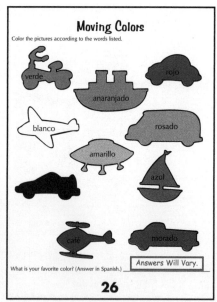

verde
rojo
anaranjado
blanco
rosado
amarillo
azul
café
morado

What is your favorite color? (Answer in Spanish.)

Answers Will Vary.

26

Color Crossword

Write the correct Spanish color words in the spaces.
Follow the English color clues.

ACROSS
3. yellow
5. purple
6. black
8. white
10. pink

DOWN
1. blue
2. red
4. orange
7. green
9. brown

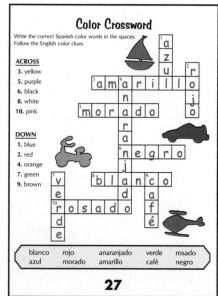

| blanco | rojo | anaranjado | verde | rosado |
| azul | morado | amarillo | café | negro |

27

Colorful Flowers

Color the flowers according to the Spanish color words shown.

28

Draw and Color

In each box, write the Spanish color word. Use the Word Bank below to help you.
Then, draw and color a picture of something that is usually that color.

Pictures Will Vary.

red is **rojo**	orange is **anaranjado**	brown is **café**
blue is **azul**	purple is **morado**	black is **negro**
green is **verde**	yellow is **amarillo**	pink is **rosado**

Which Spanish color from the Word Bank is not used above? **blanco**

Word Bank

blanco	rojo	amarillo	rosado
azul	morado	verde	negro
	anaranjado	café	

29

Butterfly Garden

Color the butterfly garden as indicated in Spanish.

30

Across the Spectrum

Write the Spanish for each clue word in the crossword puzzle.

Across
2. blue
4. brown
6. red
7. purple
8. white
9. black

Down
1. green
2. yellow
3. pink
5. orange

31

Food Words

Say each word out loud. Write the English word next to it.

queso — cheese
papa — potato
pollo — chicken
leche — milk
jugo — juice
pan — bread
ensalada — salad

Color the blocks with letters.
Do not color the blocks with numbers. What word did you find? **leche**

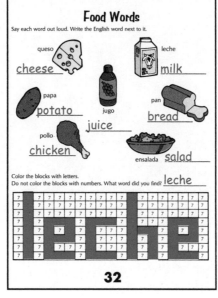

32

Food Riddles

Answer the riddles. Use the size and shape of the word blocks along with the answers at the bottom to help you.

I come from an animal. Kids like to eat my drumstick. What am I? — **pollo**

I can be full of holes. Mice like me. What am I? — **queso**

I am squeezed from fruit. Apple is a popular flavor. What am I? — **jugo**

I come from a cow. I can be regular or chocolate. What am I? — **leche**

You can eat me baked, fried, or mashed. What am I? — **papa**

You can eat me plain or with dressing. What am I? — **ensalada**

I rise while baking in an oven. What am I? — **pan**

queso   leche
papa   ensalada   pan
pollo   jugo

33

Use the Clues

Use the clues and the Word Bank at the bottom of the page to find the answers.
Do not use any answer more than once.

1. You would not eat either of these fruits until you peel them.
naranja   plátano

2. Both of these drinks have a flavor.
leche   jugo

3. You could put either of these on a sandwich.
queso   carne

4. These can be baked before eating. They all begin with the letter "p."
papa   pan   pollo

5. These two go together on a cold winter day.
sopa   sandwich

6. You use this liquid to wash this fruit.
agua   manzana

7. Which word didn't you use?
ensalada

| queso | leche | papa | jugo | pan | pollo | ensalada |
| naranja | sopa | agua | sandwich | manzana | carne | plátano |

Check off each word as you use it.

34

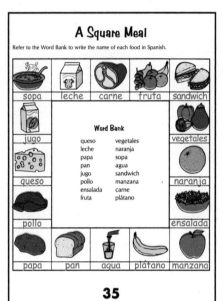

A Square Meal

Refer to the Word Bank to write the name of each food in Spanish.

sopa	leche	carne	fruta	sandwich
jugo				vegetales
queso				naranja
pollo				ensalada
papa	pan	agua	plátano	manzana

Word Bank

queso	vegetales
leche	naranja
papa	sopa
pan	agua
jugo	sandwich
pollo	manzana
ensalada	carne
fruta	plátano

35

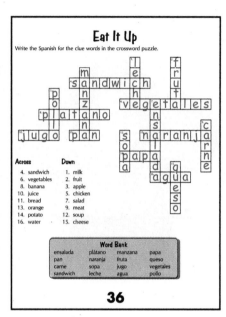

Eat It Up

Write the Spanish for the clue words in the crossword puzzle.

Across
4. sandwich
6. vegetables
8. banana
10. juice
11. bread
13. orange
14. potato
16. water

Down
1. milk
2. fruit
3. apple
5. chicken
7. salad
9. meat
12. soup
15. cheese

Word Bank

ensalada	plátano	manzana	papa
pan	naranja	fruta	queso
carne	sopa	jugo	vegetales
sandwich	leche	agua	pollo

36

Use the Clues

Answer the questions. Use the clues and the Spanish words at the bottom of the page. You may use answers more than once.

1. Both words begin with the same letter, and both animals have feathers.
pájaro   pato

2. These two animals walk and are house pets.
gato   perro

3. Both animals begin with the same letter. One quacks and the other barks.
perro   pato

4. Both of these animals like to live in the water.
pato   pez

5. These animals do not have fur or feathers.
culebra   pez

6. The first animal likes to chase and catch the second animal. They both end with the letter o.
gato   pájaro
(or perro/gato)

| gato | perro | pájaro |
| pez | pato | culebra |

37

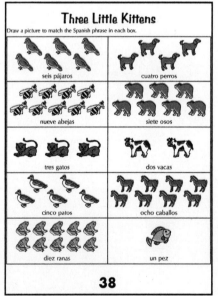

Three Little Kittens

Draw a picture to match the Spanish phrase in each box.

seis pájaros	cuatro perros
nueve abejas	siete osos
tres gatos	dos vacas
cinco patos	ocho caballos
diez ranas	un pez

38

Animal Match

Copy the Spanish word under each picture.

oso	rana	caballo	vaca
oso	rana	caballo	vaca
elefante	oveja	puerco	gallina
elefante	oveja	puerco	gallina
gato	tortuga	mariposa	dinosaurio
gato	tortuga	mariposa	dinosaurio

Write the Spanish for each animal name.

1. butterfly   mariposa
2. sheep   oveja
3. cat   gato
4. dinosaur   dinosaurio
5. chicken   gallina
6. pig   puerco

7. cow   vaca
8. bear   oso
9. elephant   elefante
10. horse   caballo
11. turtle   tortuga
12. frog   rana

39

Spanish: Grade 3

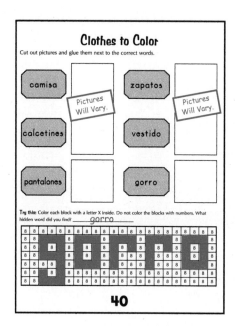

Clothes to Color

Cut out pictures and glue them next to the correct words.

camisa — Pictures Will Vary. | zapatos — Pictures Will Vary.

calcetines | vestido

pantalones | gorro

Try this: Color each block with a letter X inside. Do not color the blocks with numbers. What hidden word did you find? _gorro_

40

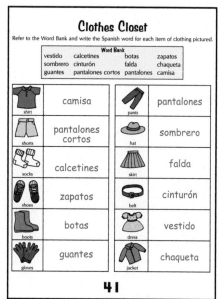

Clothes Closet

Refer to the Word Bank and write the Spanish word for each item of clothing pictured.

Word Bank

vestido, calcetines, botas, zapatos, sombrero, cinturón, falda, chaqueta, guantes, pantalones cortos, pantalones, camisa

shirt	camisa	pants	pantalones
shorts	pantalones cortos	hat	sombrero
socks	calcetines	skirt	falda
shoes	zapatos	belt	cinturón
boots	botas	dress	vestido
gloves	guantes	jacket	chaqueta

41

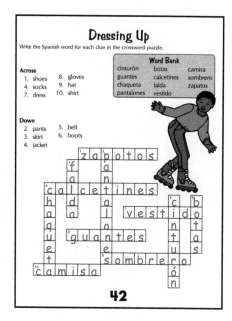

Dressing Up

Write the Spanish word for each clue in the crossword puzzle.

Across
1. shoes
4. socks
7. dress
8. gloves
9. hat
10. shirt

Down
2. pants
3. skirt
4. jacket
5. belt
6. boots

Word Bank
cinturón, botas, camisa, guantes, calcetines, sombrero, chaqueta, falda, zapatos, pantalones, vestido

¹zapotos
²f ³a
⁴calcetines
h d a l ⁶c ⁵b
a a a ⁵vestido
q u n t
⁸guantes u a
e r s
t ⁹sombrero
¹⁰camisa n

42

Matching Clothes

At the bottom of each picture, write the English word that matches the Spanish and the pictures. Write the Spanish words next to the English at the bottom of the page.

falda	zapatos	pantalones cortos	cinturón
skirt	shoes	shorts	belt
abrigo	calcetines	vestido	botas
coat	socks	dress	boots
guantes	pantalones	chaqueta	blusa
gloves	pants	jacket	blouse
gorro	sandalias	camisa	
cap	sandals	shirt	

1. skirt _falda_
2. belt _cinturón_
3. jacket _chaqueta_
4. socks _calcetines_
5. coat _abrigo_
6. shirt _camisa_
7. sandals _sandalias_
8. dress _vestido_
9. cap _gorro_
10. pants _pantalones_
11. gloves _guantes_
12. boots _botas_
13. shoes _zapatos_
14. blouse _blusa_
15. shorts _pantalones cortos_

43

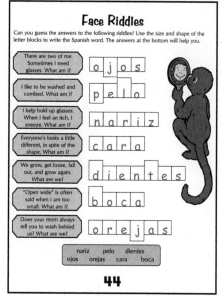

Face Riddles

Can you guess the answers to the following riddles? Use the size and shape of the letter blocks to write the Spanish word. The answers at the bottom will help you.

There are two of me. Sometimes I need glasses. What am I? — ojos

I like to be washed and combed. What am I? — pelo

I help hold up glasses. When I feel an itch, I sneeze. What am I? — nariz

Everyone's looks a little different, in spite of the shape. What am I? — cara

We grow, get loose, fall out, and grow again. What are we? — dientes

"Open wide" is often said when I am too small. What am I? — boca

Does your mom always tell you to wash behind us? What are we? — orejas

nariz, pelo, dientes, ojos, orejas, cara, boca

44

A Blank Face

Fill in the blanks with the missing letters. Use the Spanish words below to help you.

dientes, pelo, orejas, boca, ojos, nariz

nariz, pelo, dientes, ojos, orejas, cara, boca

Which word didn't you use? _cara_

Color each block that has a letter X inside. Do not color the blocks with numbers. What hidden word did you find? _boca_

45

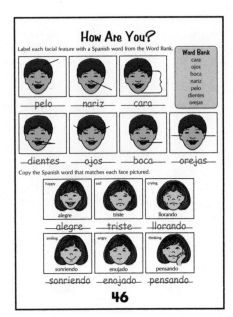

How Are You?

Label each facial feature with a Spanish word from the Word Bank.

Word Bank
cara
ojos
boca
nariz
pelo
dientes
orejas

pelo   nariz   cara

dientes   ojos   boca   orejas

Copy the Spanish word that matches each face pictured.

happy — alegre
sad — triste
crying — llorando

smiling — sonriendo
angry — enojado
thinking — pensando

46

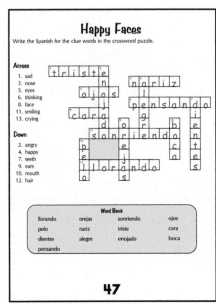

Happy Faces

Write the Spanish for the clue words in the crossword puzzle.

Across
1. sad
3. nose
5. eyes
6. thinking
8. face
11. smiling
13. crying

Down
2. angry
4. happy
7. teeth
9. ears
10. mouth
12. hair

Word Bank			
llorando	orejas	sonriendo	ojos
pelo	nariz	triste	cara
dientes	alegre	enojado	boca
pensando			

47

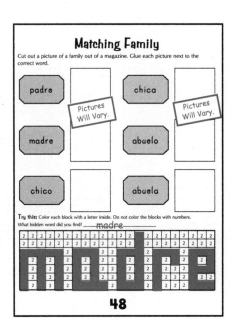

Matching Family

Cut out a picture of a family out of a magazine. Glue each picture next to the correct word.

padre — Pictures Will Vary.   chica — Pictures Will Vary.

madre   abuelo

chico   abuela

Try this: Color each block with a letter inside. Do not color the blocks with numbers. What hidden word did you find? madre

48

Family Ties

In each box, copy the Spanish word for family members.

la familia — la familia (family)
el padre — el padre (father)
la madre — la madre (mother)
el hijo — el hijo (son)
la hija — la hija (daughter)
los primos — los primos (cousins)

el hermano — el hermano (brother)
la hermana — la hermana (sister)
el tío — el tío (uncle)
la tía — la tía (aunt)
el abuelo — el abuelo (grandfather)
la abuela — la abuela (grandmother)

Write the Spanish words from above next to the English words.

sister la hermana   family la familia   father el padre
grandfather el abuelo   cousins los primos   mother la madre
grandmother la abuela   brother el hermano   daughter la hija
uncle el tío   aunt la tía   son el hijo

49

My Family

Write the Spanish word for each clue in the crossword puzzle.

Across
2. son
3. aunt
5. sister
7. grandmother
8. brother
10. cousins

Down
1. mother
2. daughter
4. family
6. grandfather
9. uncle
10. father

Word Bank			
familia	hermano	hijo	tía
primos	madre	tío	abuelo
padre	hermana	hija	abuela

50

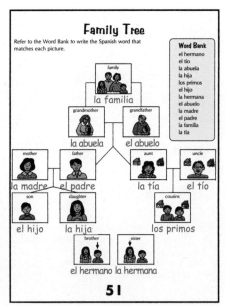

Family Tree

Refer to the Word Bank to write the Spanish word that matches each picture.

Word Bank
el hermano
el tío
la abuela
la hija
los primos
el hijo
la hermana
el abuelo
la madre
el padre
la familia
la tía

family — la familia

grandmother — la abuela   grandfather — el abuelo

mother — la madre   father — el padre   aunt — la tía   uncle — el tío

son — el hijo   daughter — la hija   cousins — los primos

brother — el hermano   sister — la hermana

51

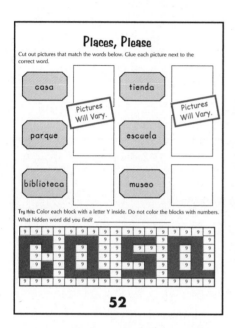

Places, Please

Cut out pictures that match the words below. Glue each picture next to the correct word.

casa — Pictures Will Vary.
tienda — Pictures Will Vary.
parque
escuela
biblioteca
museo

Try this: Color each block with a letter Y inside. Do not color the blocks with numbers. What hidden word did you find? _____

(hidden word: CASA)

52

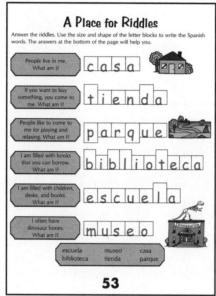

A Place for Riddles

Answer the riddles. Use the size and shape of the letter blocks to write the Spanish words. The answers at the bottom of the page will help you.

People live in me. What am I? — c a s a

If you want to buy something, you come to me. What am I? — t i e n d a

People like to come to me for playing and relaxing. What am I? — p a r q u e

I am filled with books that you can borrow. What am I? — b i b l i o t e c a

I am filled with children, desks, and books. What am I? — e s c u e l a

I often have dinosaur bones. What am I? — m u s e o

escuela	museo	casa
biblioteca	tienda	parque

53

Where Am I?

Refer to the Word Bank and write the Spanish for each place in the community pictured.

cine — museo
granja — zoológico
iglesia — biblioteca
parque — tienda
apartamento — casa
restaurante — escuela

Word Bank			
escuela	granja	biblioteca	tienda
museo	casa	apartamento	zoológico
iglesia	restaurante	cine	parque

54

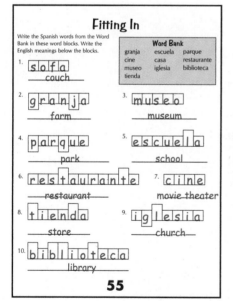

Fitting In

Write the Spanish words from the Word Bank in these word blocks. Write the English meanings below the blocks.

Word Bank		
granja	escuela	parque
cine	casa	restaurante
museo	iglesia	biblioteca
tienda		

1. s o f a — couch
2. g r a n j a — farm
3. m u s e o — museum
4. p a r q u e — park
5. e s c u e l a — school
6. r e s t a u r a n t e — restaurant
7. c i n e — movie theater
8. t i e n d a — store
9. i g l e s i a — church
10. b i b l i o t e c a — library

55

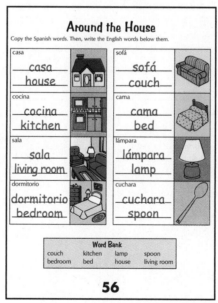

Around the House

Copy the Spanish words. Then, write the English words below them.

casa — casa / house
cocina — cocina / kitchen
sala — sala / living room
dormitorio — dormitorio / bedroom
sofá — sofá / couch
cama — cama / bed
lámpara — lámpara / lamp
cuchara — cuchara / spoon

Word Bank			
couch	kitchen	lamp	spoon
bedroom	bed	house	living room

56

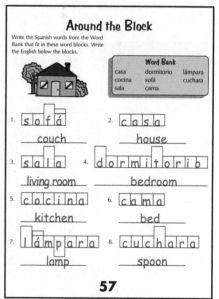

Around the Block

Write the Spanish words from the Word Bank that fit in these word blocks. Write the English below the blocks.

Word Bank		
casa	dormitorio	lámpara
cocina	sofá	cuchara
sala	cama	

1. s o f á — couch
2. c a s a — house
3. s a l a — living room
4. d o r m i t o r i o — bedroom
5. c o c i n a — kitchen
6. c a m a — bed
7. l á m p a r a — lamp
8. c u c h a r a — spoon

57

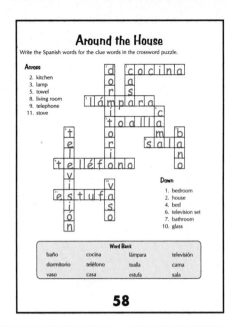

Around the House
Write the Spanish words for the clue words in the crossword puzzle.

Across
2. kitchen
3. lamp
5. towel
8. living room
9. telephone
11. stove

Down
1. bedroom
2. house
4. bed
6. television set
7. bathroom
10. glass

Crossword answers: cocina, dormitorio, casa, lámpara, c, toalla, televisión, baño, sala, teléfono, estufa, vaso

Word Bank			
baño	cocina	lámpara	televisión
dormitorio	teléfono	toalla	cama
vaso	casa	estufa	sala

58

Match Words and Pictures
Cut out pictures from a magazine and glue each picture next to the correct word.

silla
borrador
mesa

Pictures Will Vary.

lápiz
tijeras
libro

59

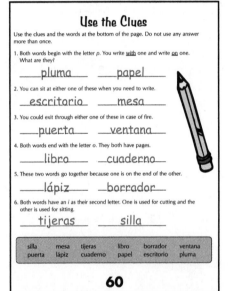

Use the Clues
Use the clues and the words at the bottom of the page. Do not use any answer more than once.

1. Both words begin with the letter *p*. You write *with* one and write *on* one. What are they?
   pluma   papel

2. You can sit at either one of these when you need to write.
   escritorio   mesa

3. You could exit through either one of these in case of fire.
   puerta   ventana

4. Both words end with the letter *o*. They both have pages.
   libro   cuaderno

5. These two words go together because one is on the end of the other.
   lápiz   borrador

6. Both words have an *i* as their second letter. One is used for cutting and the other is used for sitting.
   tijeras   silla

silla	mesa	tijeras	libro	borrador	ventana
puerta	lápiz	cuaderno	papel	escritorio	pluma

60

Around the Room
In each box, copy the Spanish word for the classroom object pictured.

silla
mesa
puerta
pluma
ventana
borrador
lápiz
cuaderno
papel
libro
escritorio
tijeras

Write the Spanish words from above next to the English words.

window ventana   chair silla   table mesa
eraser borrador   scissors tijeras   door puerta
desk escritorio   pen pluma   notebook cuaderno
paper papel   book libro   pencil lápiz

61

A Fitting Design
Write the Spanish words from the Word Bank that fit in these word blocks. Write the English meanings below the blocks.

Word Bank			
ventana	papel	pluma	puerta
borrador	silla	libro	cuaderno
escritorio	tijeras	mesa	lápiz

1. silla — chair
2. escritorio — desk
3. mesa — table
4. lápiz — pencil
5. papel — paper
6. cuaderno — notebook
7. borrador — eraser
8. libro — book
9. pluma — pen
10. puerta — door
11. ventana — window
12. tijeras — scissors

62

Classroom Clutter
Draw a picture to illustrate each of the Spanish words. Refer to the Word Bank at the bottom of the page to help you.

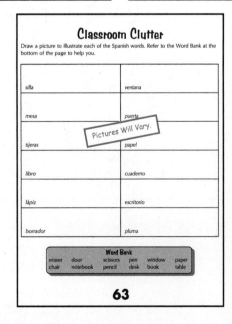

silla	ventana
mesa	puerta
tijeras	papel
libro	cuaderno
lápiz	escritorio
borrador	pluma

Pictures Will Vary.

Word Bank			
eraser	door	scissors	pen	window	paper
chair	notebook	pencil	desk	book	table

63

Show and Tell
Write the Spanish for each clue in the crossword puzzle.

Across
1. notebook
5. scissors
7. pen
8. eraser
10. pencil
11. table
12. chair

Down
2. desk
3. window
4. book
6. door
9. paper

Crossword answers: cuaderno, ventana, tijeras, pluma, borrador, lápiz, mesa, silla

Word Bank					
escritorio	mesa	libro	silla	tijeras	puerta
lápiz	ventana	borrador	cuaderno	papel	pluma

64

Published by Frank Schaffer Publications. Copyright protected.

Spanish: Grade 3